I dedicate this book to all the Entrepreneurs who throw their whole heart and soul into a dream. Without people like you, none of us would be enjoying the prosperity and life we have. Thank you!

FUNDING YOUR STARTUP

FUNDING YOUR STARTUP

Understand the Mind of the Investor and Raise Money Fast

BY TODD E. MCWHIRTER

Printed in the United States of America

First Printing, 2020

ISBN-13: 978-1-949001-45-7 print edition
ISBN-13: 978-1-949001-46-4 ebook edition

Waterside Productions
2055 Oxford Ave
Cardiff, CA 92007
www.waterside.com

TABLE OF CONTENTS

INTRODUCTION
THE MIND OF THE INVESTOR

If you're reading this, chances are you're an entrepreneur who is either seriously thinking about starting a company or who has already started one. If so, hats off to you for your vision and courage. It's you, the entrepreneur, who drives the cycle of innovation and improvement that creates prosperity around the world. It's you who will create jobs, investment opportunities and products or services that improve the way people live, work and play.

For most of us entrepreneurs, one of the hardest, most frustrating and draining parts of the job is raising the money to launch the vision. Sitting down with potential investors, sharing your dream and getting a "maybe" or a "no, thanks" over and over feels like a total waste of time, and can be extremely disheartening.

I have been an investor in startups for almost 25 years. During this time, I have analyzed well over 350 startups, raising over $14 million for both my ideas and others. This adventure has brought me both wild success and bankruptcy. I was able to retire because of startups at age 36, lost almost everything through startups at age

44, and could have chosen to be retired again through startups at age 53. I have learned the hard way.

To be sure, I am not claiming to be some connected Silicon Valley venture capital guy or even some guru angel investor. I am a simple man who, as a sales manager of young salespeople, happened to stumble into an investing career almost by accident. I started off knowing nothing about the Startup world. I jumped in fairly blind, believing only that I was backing extremely hardworking people with grit and character.

Through my own struggles in the startup world, I figured some things out. Why do potential investors say "no" to great ideas? What helps potential investors say "yes?" Why do some of the greatest ideas fail? Why do mediocre ideas sometimes succeed?

I realized that my struggle to find the answers to these questions could be of great value to entrepreneurs with solid ideas who are struggling to raise the capital they need to launch. Although I make my living as an investor, writing and consulting to help entrepreneurs get their ideas off the ground has become one of my passions.

After reading these pages you will know what I like to call "the mind of the investor." Understanding how investors think is the first step to solving this money-raising problem. If you implement the advice you find in the chapters of this book, money-raising is more likely to become achievable and your new enterprise will be better positioned for success.

This is not meant to be an extensive education on every aspect of raising money, but instead an overview of the process that will help you understand how we investors think.

Imagine not dreading the money-raising stage of the startup process. Imagine yourself sitting down with potential investors and getting "yes" after "yes" instead of "no" and "maybe." Imagine being able to launch your vision with the financial runway you need to make your vision take flight. Imagine making your investors such a great return that you have their confidence for life.

These chapters are simple. Some of the advice may strike you as obvious, but you would be surprised by how many of the new business plans that cross my desk fail to cover these fundamentals.

For clarity, when I mention *business plan*, I don't mean the old-school 100-page business plan bound in one of those old paper binders. What I see mostly these days is a "pitch deck," but even a good pitch deck is not enough. What I mean by *business plan* is a REAL PLAN. A plan that covers all the details, helping us investors feel confident that you are not winging it.

This Plan will of course include a pitch deck, pro formas, your exit strategy and many other things. Most likely it will be digital and not all in one paper binder. However, I decided to use the old-school phrase *business plan* because I still feel this encompasses the details needed to give investors the confidence to invest. Maybe I'm trying to bring the *business plan* back with a spruced-up idea of what that looks like. This book can serve as a guide for such a plan.

Raising money is like selling anything: You need to find your audience's need and fill it. I will share with you how many investors think so you can clearly commit to what they need and raise the money to fuel your dream.

Thanks for reading!

Todd E McWhirter
FundingYourStartup.com

CHAPTER 1
THE IDEA

Everyone starting a company has a great idea. The saying, "Ideas are a dime a dozen" is, unfortunately, true. Your idea alone is worth less than one penny. Instinctively, you know this. How many great ideas have been tossed around over a few beers? You know that what gives any idea great value is the implementation of the idea. It's the implementer that we invest in much more than the idea.

Raising money is selling. A good idea might get you a meeting with a potential investor, but to get money, you must show a great deal more. First, you must show the potential investor that you have a clear understanding of your idea — what your exact product or service is and what problem it solves. Second, you must show that you understand your competition very well – why customers will choose you over the others. Third, your idea has to have been tested. One way or another, you must prove that the idea sells, not just in theory, but in reality. Fourth, you must show that you have the skill set and right team to implement, market and scale your business 10- to 50-fold.

Clear Understanding of Your Idea

Many entrepreneurs are idea people. They think of a great idea every week, if not more. It then becomes a question of focus and clarity. Investors need to know that your idea is fully baked. I have sat down with many entrepreneurs who have a new and different revenue stream each time we meet. Although I admire their creativity, not having your plan locked down and cemented for the initial launch is, in my opinion, a plan that is still in the oven, and therefore, not ready for money-raising.

Identity is important as well. What problem does your business solve? What is your target market? What is your unique edge? What is your mission statement and how does your business fulfill this? These questions should be easy to answer for the entrepreneur.

I think of an investment that I made a while back in a company that could and should have been YouTube, but they were never able to clearly articulate their identity. They had so many good ideas centered around video on the internet and so many revenue-stream rabbit trails that none worked in the end. They had an identity problem, and therefore a strategy problem. Even huge companies like Sears, for example, are now suffering from an identity problem. They're not Wal-Mart, they're not Home Depot and they're not Macy's. Beyond their identity as a super retailer, they're trying to be a mix of all three of these successful competitors and, I believe, struggling and failing in the attempt.

Before you get in front of an investor, you should have a clear concept of what problem you are solving (identity) and be able to show a laser focus on your core revenue stream.

Know Your Competition

This may seem obvious, but what investors need to believe is that you not only know your competition, but know exactly what differentiates you from your competition. Moreover, investors need to know what your specific plan is for keeping an edge above your competition. Not doing all your homework in this area and not having a realistic plan for how your business will attract customers (regardless of your competition) can dramatically hinder your money-raising efforts and, even worse, dramatically hinder your chances of success.

I remember doing some internet research after sitting down with an entrepreneur. Within 10 minutes I found major competitors that were not mentioned in his business plan. Not only that, I saw blogs smearing the industry. Although smears on the internet can mean nothing and everyone has competition, it was that the entrepreneur did not bring this up first that made me doubt his preparation and integrity.

Your idea isn't worth investing in until you've set it alongside probable competitors and thoroughly analyzed where you can beat them and where you can't.

Test the Idea

Testing the idea is critical. Of course you love your idea. Of course your friends love your idea. You know it will work. But without a real test, the idea, no matter how good it sounds, won't give investors the confidence to write that check. You must test your idea. To be fair, your idea might have been tested by others if you are entering the market as a differentiated competitor rather than something completely new and different. But even so, some sort of test showing that customers actually would pay for or prefer your differentiator is a must.

What constitutes a sufficient test varies immensely depending on your market and product. The point of this section is to encourage you to make sure that whatever test you choose is as close to a real transaction as possible.

A few thoughts on testing your idea:

- Don't use your friends or family for the testing.
- Make sure your test is done in the same way your actual sales after launch will be done. For example, if you plan on selling a product in retail stores, convincing a small retail store to try out your product is the way to go. Saying "I would

buy something" and actually buying something are very different things.

Providing quantifiable proof of concept is critical to earning an investor's confidence.

Prove You Can Implement and Scale

In my many meetings with entrepreneurs, I often see amazing ideas with pro forma demonstrating revenue scaling to the millions. All this is good. But when I ask specific questions about how they plan on building a culture and team, or what systems they can implement to improve their sales process or what plan they have for creating loyalty with their customer base, I often get a blank stare.

Many times, the answer I get is something like, "we are still working those things out." Needless to say, I pass on those opportunities.

Without the proper skill set and understanding of how to implement and scale your business, it's highly unlikely that your business will grow past the "Mom & Pop" size. Mom & Pop businesses can be great, and are many times my preference as a consumer, but usually don't have outside shareholders. For investors to write you a check, you must prove beyond a doubt that you have the skill set to build a company culture and team, the foresight to implement systems, and proper understanding of marketing and sales.

Creating a Culture and Building a Team

It takes a team to grow a company. It takes a successful culture to build a team. And it takes a talented, committed leader to create a successful culture. The investors know this, so taking the time to brag about your team is a good idea. Describe in detail how you plan on retaining your key people. Describe what you have done in the past that proves to the investors that you understand how important your team is and that you know how to keep them focused and excited. In your business plan, outline your "Business Philosophy" and describe your vision regarding how you plan on treating your customers, your employees and your strategic partners.

Implementing Systems

These days, it's my belief that every company has to become a tech company. One of my investments is a co-working space company. Another one sells ground transportation. I have invested in a large liquor store. How are these tech companies? My point is that in this internet age, if you don't know how to implement technology into your business process, the goal of scaling your business is not much more than a pipe dream. In the beginning stages, every startup I have invested in starts off rather chaotic. Every one that has succeeded has been able to use technology to implement systems and processes to move from the chaotic stage to something much more efficient. Demonstrating that you have the know-how or have people with the know-how to implement systems and processes within your selling cycle is paramount.

Marketing and Sales

Once funded, this area should occupy a massive percentage of your time. For our purposes here, I will only briefly touch on what investors will be looking for.

Marketing and sales require different approaches, yet both have the shared goal of capturing new business and retaining existing business. Your potential investors will want to see a detailed plan for each, showing how they work.

Your investors will want to know that you have a plan for new customers, existing customers and customers yet to convert. Each of these should be treated differently, with action steps to "touch" each one in a way that moves them toward conversion or repeat business.

Each of these steps and tools has costs and conversion metrics. In the beginning stages, much of this will be projection, but showing that you understand this cost-per-lead concept and that your pro forma is based on working knowledge will go a long way to securing investors.

Proving you can implement and scale your business takes more than numbers in the pro forma. You must back those numbers up with working knowledge of how you will build a team, how you will implement systems, and a methodical and measurable marketing and sales plan.

Chapter 2
The Numbers

Investors are numbers people by nature. Ideas are fun to kick around, but if potential investors don't see and understand the numbers — all the numbers — they most likely will not be investing in your company. The following is a list of basics that should go into your business plan — basics that are especially important to investors. In many of the investment opportunities that I passed on, I found the entrepreneurs' plans consistently weak in these areas.

Use of Funds

Investors take pride in their investing decisions. It's likely they have looked at many companies and heard lots of good ideas. It's only natural that they take special interest in what you plan on doing with the money you raise. Not having your "Use of Funds" section itemized can be a huge burden on your money-raising efforts. Just as there are red flags that you must avoid, there are "green flags" you can create by adding detail and specifics.

First, the red flags. Using the newly raised money for high salaries will not help your money-raising efforts. Your personal salary will be looked at closely; the lower, the better, and in the beginning, it's best if you pay yourself with some sort of bonus for hitting specific milestones. If you must use some of the money to keep your team going, draws against future commissions are the best way to incentivize. Of course, there are certain roles that must be salaried, but the important thing is that you show the investors that you are keeping the salaries as low as possible until the business can support small, incremental and justifiable raises. Your key people should be incentivized with stock options, profit sharing or some other path besides high salaries. I will cover this further in the *Employee Option Pool* chapter.

Other red flags in the Use of Funds section that should be avoided are anything that can be looked at as a luxury: High-rent offices, expensive décor or any other item that might be viewed as unnecessary. Of course, some companies must have these luxury items because of the nature of the business, but the point is to make sure that every item in your Use of Funds is absolutely defensible for the purpose of getting you to break-even. Investors will be keenly attuned to your burn rate and any money you are burning that is not a "must" will be looked at as wasted cash.

Some green flags that can help strengthen your Use of Funds section are areas that have lasting value or are part of the cost of goods. Using money to create intellectual property such as software programs that improve company systems is a good thing. Spending money on inventory, patents or other intellectual property may also look good to investors. Think in terms of creating real lasting value with the money you raise. Think about spending money on things that will help you save money in the long run and help you produce sales. It's always good to show how the money you raise will help you hit specific milestones.

Before you show your plan to an investor, take a hard look at your Use of Funds and evaluate each item as to whether it could be seen as a frill or something that will create lasting value and make money. Make sure your use of funds gets you to specific goals or milestones.

Return on Investment (ROI)

Much of this topic I will cover in greater detail in *The Exit* chapter, but suffice it to say, there isn't anything that investors care more about than their ROI. Entrepreneurs sometimes forget that the business idea is their baby — not the investor's baby. The investor is usually investing for one reason and one reason only: They believe that this investment will provide them a big return on their money. Of course, there are investors that use other criteria, but I can assure you that if your ROI is weak, not realistic or has seemingly higher-than-normal risk, your money-raising will be a constant struggle.

Investors are looking for an opportunity that has potential for 10 to 50 times their money, and here's why: They know that the majority of their startup investments will fail. Of course, as the entrepreneur, you need to aim for success and present a plan that maximizes your odds, but the brutal fact remains: 9 out of 10 startup companies are likely to fail. Investors have to plan on several zero-ROI scenarios. The ones that make it have to make up for the ones that don't. True, this may feel unfair to the entrepreneur, yet this is the reality.

Another important concept to bear in mind is that if your company is one of the winners, there is a good chance it will still take twice as long, cost twice as much and return half the amount that is in your projections.

Regardless, you should resist the temptation to account for this by creating unrealistic figures. Anything unrealistic is an obvious deal-breaker that the seasoned investor will spot a mile away. Their checkbooks will stay in their pockets.

So, your task is not an easy one: You must show investors a realistic 10X- to 50X-return on their money in a three- to seven-year period.

There are exceptions to the 10X- to-50X-ROI rule, but not many. Some examples of these exceptions would include:

- companies launched by extremely seasoned entrepreneurs who have a proven track record achieving solid returns for their investors;
- ones that present a less risky business concept, such as some real estate deals;
- those that offer collateral for the investors; or
- companies that have proven concepts that are already succeeding and need money to specifically scale.

Another good way to raise money without such a high ROI is to build in a creative way to get the investors their principal back quickly. I will cover this in more detail in *The Offering* chapter.

Most investors want to see a potential 10X- to 50X-return on their startup investment. With a realistic plan to get there, you're on the way toward attracting investors.

<u>Valuation</u>

I will now address post-money valuation — the valuation of your company after investment or financing — in hopes of helping you structure your thinking with your investor in mind. The formula looks like this: Pre-money valuation + amount of money raised = post-money valuation. For example, if you are offering 30% of your company for $300K, then your post-money valuation is $1 million. In this example, your pre-money valuation would be $700K. $700K + $300K (raised) = $1M. The investors then take 30% for $300K, so they are investing in a post-money valuation of $1M.

For our use, then, I am going to use the term "valuation" interchangeably with "post-money valuation," since this is the way most entrepreneurs and investors calculate valuation.

If you have ever seen the show *Shark Tank*, you have probably watched someone lose a deal because they are out of touch with reality regarding valuation.

Valuation of your company — or, in some cases, the valuation of your business plan — is really like selling anything. The market (your potential investors) will dictate the value of your stock or the value of X percentage of the LLC. Valuate it too high and you will not attract investors; valuate it too low and you will sell more of your company than was needed. The trick, of course, is to hit that sweet spot where you raise the money you need quickly and feel good about what is left over for you and your team.

Coming up with this number is definitely more of an art than a science. And just like a good piece of art takes a mixture of multiple factors — lighting, colors and texture — a good valuation also must also be composed of well-chosen elements. These factors are:

- The ROI that will attract investors.
- The amount of money you need to raise.
- The amount of equity in the company you are willing to give away.
- A realistic break-even strategy and exit strategy that makes the above points work.

Your job is to blend these factors together in such a way that they all speak to the motivations of both the investor(s) and the founder(s).

Here are some examples of these factors in action.

❧ ❧ ❧

Let's suppose you need $300K to get your company to break-even and beyond, and your realistic exit is a $10M sale. Let's also assume you are in the early stages and therefore, in order to attract investors, it may be helpful to target a 20X ROI.

$300K initial investment x 20 = $6M to the investors.

If the company's exit sale is $10M, the investors end up with $6M or 60% of the exit price.

So, a $300K investment would need to purchase 60% of the company in this scenario, making the company valuation come in at $500K.

$300K/$500K = 60%

That may or may not work for you, but that is how the numbers play out. However, these numbers can be massaged to fit your situation. For example, you can lower your initial raise by a $100K, get things off the ground with $200K, and raise the other $100K at a higher valuation once you have proven the model. Or perhaps you can attract investors with a 15X possible return and make the math work that way. The key is hitting the sweet spot, where investors are excited about the ROI based on the real and perceived risk, and at the same time you, the entrepreneur, feel good about the ownership you are selling.

⚜ ⚜ ⚜

If, however, you only need $200K to kick off your company and hit break-even and beyond, and your realistic exit was a $10 million sale, keeping the same 20X return; the puzzle looks different.

$200K initial investment x 20 = $4M to the investors.

If the company's exit sale is $10M, the investors end up with $4M or 40% of the exit price.

That means you would be offering 40% of your company and giving it the same valuation of $500K.

With this scenario, you can move things around if you would like, as long as you ensure that the perceived risk at your stage meets the perceived ROI in the mind of the investors. For example, set the valuation at $600K and sell 33% of your company for $200K, giving investors a potential 16X or 17X return. Or, add a preferred return (which I will talk about later) to your offering and sell only 20% of your company for the $200K making the upside a 10X return, but the downside is less risky with the preferred return in place.

⚜ ⚜ ⚜

Let's take an example involving dividends:

You need to raise $120K to get your company to break-even and beyond. You also believe you need to provide a 15X ROI over seven years to attract investors.

Let's also assume you are willing to sell 40% of the company to do this.

$120K/valuation needs to equal 40%; therefore, your valuation is $300K.

Although this valuation might sound low, this is a common scenario for new entrepreneurs with an idea still in the initial business plan stage.

Now let's look at the dividend schedule to hit the seven-year 15X goal with a $120K investment: $120K x 15 = $1.8M. The math then shows a need to distribute $1.8M total over seven years to hit the 15X ROI for your investors.

Your task is to create a realistic dividend schedule that can provide this sort of return. Continuing the assumption, you sold 40% of the company to raise the 120K, it might look like this:

1st year predict $0 total distributable profit
2nd year predict $200K total distributable profit,
        40% of $200K = $80K to investors.
3rd year predict $500K total distributable profit,
        40% of $500K = $200K to investors.
4th year predict $700K total distributable profit,
        40% of $700K = $280K to investors.
5th year predict $900K total distributable profit,
        40% of $900K = $360K to investors.
6th year predict $1M total distributable profit,
        40% of $1M = $400K to investors.
7th year predict $1.2M total distributable profit,
        40% of $1.2M = $480K to investors.
Total paid out to investors = $1.8M, representing a
        15X return over seven years.

❖   ❖   ❖

You absolutely must stay grounded in what's realistic. As I write this, I can see the ease of changing numbers to make any valuation you want work very well on paper. It's not that simple. If you're trying to spin things that you know are not realistic, even a moderately savvy investor will walk away.

So, what do you do if the math just doesn't work?

If you can't, in clear conscience, show an exit strategy that provides an exciting ROI based on the amount of money you need to raise and the amount of the company you are willing to sell, what do you do?

You are in a valuation dilemma.

If you find yourself in this situation, you only have a few honest options. One option is to re-think your business plan, finding some way to either change the exit or the amount of money you need. The other option is to keep your day job until you can prove your model with real revenue by creating a break-even company before you raise money. Raising money to scale rather than to prove your model will fetch a much greater valuation, making it much easier to make the puzzle work. A third option is to get creative with your offering, which leads us into our next chapter.

Valuation must artfully strike the balance between expected value for the entrepreneur and the investor, while remaining wholly credible.

Chapter 3

The Offering

The offering and the exit are the front door and the back door for investors. Investors enter your company via the offering and leave your company via the exit, and their all-important ROI is what connects the two. A creative offering and an exciting and realistic exit strategy will do wonders for raising money. In this chapter, I will cover a few highlights and ideas for your offering.

The business plan has all the sexy stuff in it, whereas the offering is usually full of legal jargon written up by an attorney to protect you from future lawsuits. This being the case, there are still ways to make the offering quite appealing and exciting. Once you have decided upon the main elements of your deal, you will need to have an attorney craft them into a proper legal document.

For our purposes here, let me first give you a couple of the most common ways of structuring an offering. Then I will cover a few ideas that you can use to sweeten the deal and turn a "maybe" into a "yes!"

Straight Equity Offering

One of the most common approaches is a straight equity offering, where X dollars purchase Y amount of equity. This can be a percentage of an LLC or a specific amount of shares at a specific price. This type of offering means that you have settled on a specific valuation for your company.

Although this may be obvious, it's important that you are prepared to answer the grilling you'll receive about how you arrived at the valuation. As discussed earlier, you must be able to defend your company's valuation with realistic growth numbers and realistic exit scenarios.

A straight equity deal is the most traditional way to raise money. Many investors will only invest this way because they want to know what they are getting for their money.

Convertible Notes

Another way to structure your offering is with Convertible Notes. This approach will offer investors a Promissory Note at an interest rate. This Note gives the investors rights (or the company rights depending on how you set it up) to convert the original principal invested plus interest accrued into equity at a later date.

The advantage for the entrepreneur is that they don't have to settle in on an exact valuation until the Convertible Notes come due which is usually triggered by a bigger money raise (typically called Series A financing) down the road. This allows you to use the money raised to create more value, and hopefully sell less of your company to investors. This may sound too good to be true, so let me break down a few sobering points surrounding Convertible Notes.

Many investors (including myself) prefer straight equity because we want to know what percentage our money is purchasing at the time we invest. That said, you must have a very good and justifiable reason to be using a Convertible Note to raise the money you need.

The only good and justifiable reason that I am aware of for using a Convertible Note is if you know that you will need to raise millions of dollars to take your idea from business plan to wild success. When all you have is an idea on paper, it's extremely difficult to justify a valuation much more than $1 million and even that can be a stretch when you have no revenue to date. Therefore, if you need a million or more dollars to launch your idea, a Convertible Note offering might be your best bet – pushing the valuation decision off into the future when the business is further along.

This is, however, a difficult pitch for investors to get excited about. The idea needs to be a potential "game changer" or in a category where typical exits are extremely high. In other words, the risk of investing in a Convertible Note needs to match the potential upside.

This happens often when the idea is a tech category, for example, creating an App that needs to build a huge user base before it can begin to implement a revenue stream. Something like this would be a good and justifiable reason to use a Convertible Note for your offering strategy.

If this sounds like the way you want to go, there are three important factors that need consideration:

- Setting a *cap* on the future valuation.
- Setting a *discount* from the future valuation.

- Determining the *interest rate* on the Note.

The more generous you are with these factors, the quicker you will raise the money. Let me explain.

Let's suppose you have an idea that you believe is a game changer. You have zero revenue but have an extremely detailed plan on how you will develop and launch your idea. You think you're going to need $2M or $3M to hit your goal, but also think you can get off the ground and prove the model with $500K. Being in the business plan stage and knowing you're going to need future rounds of big money creates the need for the Convertible Note, but how do you sell this concept? Answer: Caps, discounts and a healthy interest rate.

An example would look like this:

A 9% APR Convertible Note with a cap valuation of $3 million and/or a 20% discount from the Series A round valuation, whichever is less.

The way that would play out looks like this:

The $500K initial seed round would be on the books as a Promissory Note with a 9% APR that accrues over time. The Note converts to equity either in three years OR when the Series A round is raised, whichever comes sooner. The Series A round (usually venture capital money) "sets" the future valuation. Let's suppose two years after the original Note, you find a VC firm who invests $1 million at a $5 million post money valuation – in other words, they purchase 20% of the company for $1 million. The original $500K then converts at either the cap of a $3 million valuation or 20% discount from the $5 million valuation, whichever is less. In this case the cap ($3M) is less than the 20% discount ($4M). So $500K plus two years of 9% interest ($500K x 1.09 x 1.09) or $594K would convert at a $3 million valuation, which would represent another 19.8% of the company. All said and done at this point you have sold around 40% of your company and raised $1.5 million. Not a bad start, provided you have executed on your plan.

Convertible Notes are a good way to go if you need big money and are still in the business plan stage. They are certainly harder to sell than straight equity, but if your idea has huge upside and you're realistic and generous with the cap, the discount and the interest rate, this might be your best option.

With either offering approach (straight equity or Convertible Notes), understand that although you are confident that your business will wildly succeed, the investor is naturally looking at all the things that can go wrong. Sweetening up the deal, therefore, can be the nudge that helps them write that check. These sweeteners include warrants, options, personal guarantees/collateral, and my favorite, preferred returns.

<u>Warrants and Options</u>
Offering warrants or options to those who invest is a very nice incentive and is commonly understood in the investment community. Effectively, this is an opportunity for

the investor to increase their ownership of the company in the future, at a set price. This motivating structure can be set up with C-corps, S-corps and LLCs.

There are endless variations of warrants and options, and many others have written extensively on this subject. For our purposes – helping you understand the mind of the investor in order to raise money fast – I will hit the basic concepts.

Warrants (used by C-corps or S-corps) – Within the context of startups, warrants offer the right to purchase a specific number of shares of a corporation at a set price within a set time frame. These shares are created in the future when the warrant is executed, diluting the current shareholders pro-rata. Example: A warrant offering 1,000 shares (representing, say, 1% of the company) at $10/share (often the same price they paid for the original investment) that must be exercised on or before (say, four years) from the date of the warrant, or the warrant will expire.

Options (used by C-corps, S-corps or LLCs) – Within the context of startups, options are the right to purchase a specific number of existing shares or percentage of existing equity at a set price within a set time frame. With C-corps, these shares are either already "set aside" in an option pool, and with S-corps or LLCs, they are merely a commitment from one person (usually the founder) to sell to another person (usually a strategic investor). Example: An option offered to a strategic investor that lasts for (say, five years) the ability to purchase (say, 2%) of the founder's ownership (or out of the option pool) at the same price per share or per percent they originally invested.

The main point surrounding this structure is finding the win-win with regard to the price of the warrant/option, the size of the warrant/option and the time frame to exercise the warrant/option. Obviously, the investor wants the lowest price, the largest amount of equity, and the longest possible time frame, while the entrepreneur wants a higher price, wants to give as little equity away as possible, with a shorter time frame. Finding the right mix is the trick. You want to raise money fast, but not have to give options to everyone and anyone to get that done.

I would recommend you assess who the investor is and try to determine if warrants or options makes sense. For example, some investors can lead to an entire group of other investors, as they might be part of Investor Clubs and such. Others might be seasoned in areas that could be strategic as you go forward. Using options or warrants to attract smart and connected investors and/or advisors can be invaluable.

The entrepreneur can use warrants and options to incentivize an investor to take action. Use them wisely and they can open doors to more investors and help you build a solid Advisory Team.

Personal Guarantees or Collateral
Having some sort of collateral or signing a personal guarantee to go alongside the offering is another way I have

seen entrepreneurs turn "maybe" investors into "yes" investors.

As an example of collateral, offering shares in some real estate as a fallback if the company fails can be a real way to lower the risk and attract the money you need. Putting up your car, your boat or similar property can go a long way toward building confidence with early investors, even though your collateral might not fully cover the principal invested.

Personal guarantees can be used without or in addition to collateral. Either way, they can show the investor that you are in this thing come hell or high water.

These are very risky scenarios for you, so seek a good advisor or attorney that can help you understand the risks involved before you venture into offering collateral or signing a personal guarantee.

Putting your own property on the line and/or signing a personal guarantee to attract investor dollars can generate the additional confidence that gets investors to decide in your favor. Consult an advisor or attorney so that you know all the risks.

Preferred Returns

This final sweetener, in my opinion, is a slam dunk. I have seen how this approach motivates investors and draws checkbooks out of pockets. This is exactly what it sounds like: Pay the investors back their principal before the founders personally enjoy any profit out of the company. This might be hard to swallow at first, but it can do wonders to demonstrate your desire to make sure that your investors do very well.

As with everything else, there are a variety of ways to structure a Preferred Return; I will speak to a few basics regarding the "how," and equally important, the "why."

The How:

If your company is a C-corp, the most common way to set up Preferred Returns is using the strategy of offering Preferred Stock to your investors (as opposed to Common Stock). Preferred Stock has many potential rights, preferences and privileges that you can choose ranging from Preferred Returns, to specific voting rights, to anti-dilution clauses, etc. For our purposes, I will focus on the Preferred Return privilege, usually called *Liquidation Preference.*

Liquidation Preference is the ability to recover the initial investment upon the liquidation of the company before holders of Common Stock receive any value for their stock. There are basically three ways to set up a *Liquidation Preference*, ranging from most beneficial to the investor (called *Participating Preferred Stock*), to most beneficial to the entrepreneur (called *Straight* or *Non-Participating Preferred Stock*). The third way is an attempt to meet in the middle (called *Capped* or *Partial Participating Preferred Stock*).

In a nutshell, you have a decision as to how generous you want to be. *Participating Preferred Stock* allows the investor to get their money back first (plus accrued dividends) before common stock holders receive any money. Plus, they participate in the pro-rata distribution when you exit. The *Non-Participating Preferred Stock* is just that. These investors get their money back first (plus accrued dividends) but *do not* get to participate in the pro-rata exit. The *Capped* or *Partial Participating Preferred Stock* is the middle ground. It allows for the investors to receive money back first (plus accrued dividends) and partially participating, where the investors get to enjoy the exit up to a certain capped return.

If your company is an S-corp or LLC, you can accomplish the similar range of Preferred Returns, however you would *not* be using Preferred Stock to do so. S-corps, by definition, only have one type of stock, and LLCs of course do not have stock, but rather investors simply own a percentage of the LLC. So how than do we set up a Preferred Return? Think in terms of concept.

With LLCs and S-corps everything is spelled out in the Operating Agreement and signed and sealed with everyone's signature. The simplest way I have seen the concept of Preferred Returns successfully implemented with LLCs and S-Corps is with the use of loans. An investor would, for example, loan an LLC $50K with zero interest (or low interest) to be paid back on or before year five of the loan. Rather than accepting an interest rate as consideration, they would accept equity in the LLC. This structure accomplishes the goal: The investor gets their money back plus gets to participate in the exit with the equity they "bought" by forgoing any interest (or by accepting a low interest rate).

The Why:

I recently was involved in a company where they needed $90K to kick off their vision for the company. The founder wanted to raise the money fast and I suggested a Preferred Return. It was an LLC, so they included the Preferred Return loan language in the Operating Agreement. The nuts and bolts looked like this: All $90K was set up as a zero-interest loan, to be paid back to the investors before any of the founding team could enjoy any distribution of profits. If fact, they went a step further. The founder limited his salary to $5K per month until the $90K was paid back. Talk about motivation to get the investors whole! By doing this, they were able to raise the $90K in less than one month and get a much larger valuation than they would have without this structure.

The Why is very clear to me. By limiting the downside for investors, you accomplish several things:

- First, this clearly demonstrates to investors that you understand the level of risk they are taking. You put investors' money first in line, which speaks volumes.
- Second, your able to raise money much faster. When an investor can see that the odds of him or her at least getting whole are pretty good, they naturally feel more comfortable investing, speeding up the money-raising efforts. This of course allows you to stay focused on building the business.

- Third, with a Preferred Return structure in place, you can justify a larger valuation, therefore selling less equity than if this structure was not in place. This is especially true when you are merely a business plan, or at a very early stage in the business with little or no revenue.

Most lawyers will naturally try to "protect you" and steer you away from this concept. And to be sure, there are a few things to be aware of when making this decision.

When you offer a Preferred Return to your initial investors, it's more than likely that you will need to continue this structure on future rounds creating a larger principal to be paid back first. Also, the second round investors might not like that you have this structure in place, possibly making the second round more difficult to close.

If you are only planning on one or two rounds of fund raising, and the rounds are relatively small ($100K to $500K) it's not that hard to make this structure work. If you plan on many rounds, relatively big rounds, and possibly using a venture capital firm, you might want to listen to those lawyers – raising millions and millions of dollars can make the Preferred Return concept difficult to work. Do the math.

The devil is in the details, so once you know what you want to accomplish, hire a good attorney and accountant to help you set everything up properly. If they say you can't do Preferred Returns, find another attorney or accountant. If they advise against using Preferred Returns, listen and assess the pros and cons carefully.

The Preferred Return concept is by nature very generous! The pros are that it helps you accomplish your goals of raising money fast and getting a valuation that helps everyone on the founding team stay motivated. Get the right counsel, as Preferred Returns can create some cons to consider regarding their affect on future rounds.

Summary

There is no right or wrong way to offer incentives; however, if they don't motivate, they are not worth the legal work required to write up the deal. And, of course, if they are too good, they either cause suspicion or end up costing you more equity than was necessary.

Finding the balance is a function of the market. The investors will need a better deal if the perceived risk is higher and will accept a lesser deal if the perceived risk is lower. I have had people ask me many times, "How long will this money-raising process take?" Assuming you can make the case to investors that your business is viable, my answer is simple: "It depends on how sweet the deal is." These are big decisions, so consulting with other entrepreneurs, other angel investors and of course, your accountants and legal counsel can help you navigate this process.

Chapter 4
The Exit

Using the analogy that the offering is the front door and the exit is the back door might help you understand why a detailed, clear and realistic exit is critical. If the investors do not understand and believe that they will get out the back door, they will never, ever enter the front door. Remember that when investors enter the front door of your company through your offering, they become minority shareholders in a non-marketable company. They basically give up control of their money and are largely at the mercy of the board's decisions. They are stuck in the house until the back door is unlocked — until your exit strategy plays out.

Understanding the investors' situation should help you understand the importance of your exit strategy. I have sat down with entrepreneurs who are very sharp, have great ideas, have a great plan to get off the ground and deliver on big revenue numbers, yet offered weak or vague investor exit scenarios. Remember: For investors, their money is their product. They need to see and understand how their money flows in and out just as surely as you need to see your product and service flow cycle. It's easy to get excited about your product and how it's going to sell like crazy and forget the simple fact that investors, although they certainly care about your product, care much more about your plan to get them a healthy ROI.

There are really only four ways that investors can get their money back in a startup company: Dividends, a sale of the company, the company buying back its own stock or taking the company public. I will briefly cover each one, focusing on how they relate to four themes: Profit, realism, detail and clarity.

A **profitable** company serves each exit strategy well. Potential investors must believe the exit is **real** or they will not invest. An exit strategy without sufficient **detail** seems more like a wish than a strategy. **Clarity** is a must because confused potential investors never invest.

Dividends
Dividends are a distribution of profits. This is the most real and believable scenario. There is no "pie in the sky" plan for dividends. Dividends can make you and your investors extremely wealthy. A dividend-producing company makes all other exit strategies possible. Dividends keep you focused on what is most important to the investors: Profit. Focusing on profit alongside revenue is, in my opinion, optimal for getting a "yes" from an investor. A profit-focused entrepreneur has to think of both sales and expenses, must be numbers-oriented, and must show how they will keep the company running lean — all of which

investors love to hear. If dividends are going to be your main exit plan for your investors, there are a few things to keep in mind as you prepare this part of your business plan.

As mentioned in Chapter 2, *The Numbers*, your job is a tough one. You need to strike the balance between realistic and exciting dividend projections. Investors, therefore, need to believe three things to trust in your dividend exit strategy:

1. That your expenses/costs are **real** and that you have a **detailed** and **clear** plan to keep them lean.
2. That your revenue projections are **real** and that you have a **detailed** and **clear** plan to scale.
3. That you are committed to dividends and you have made this **clear** and **real** by putting yourself and your board of directors in the same situation as your investors. I will cover this in more detail in the next chapter titled *Same Page Philosophy.*

I remember sitting down with a young entrepreneur who had a great business plan. It looked to me like he had what it would take to succeed. When we got to his expenses, I noticed a few items that he had not thought about. When I brought up that he might have forgotten a few costs, he said that this was his first stab at the potential expenses and that he would need to take another look. Needless to say, I did not invest, as it warned me that realism was not yet a focus. I have turned down many startup opportunities because the sales figures were not, in my opinion, grounded in realism.

One company that I did invest in had a section in his business plan titled *How Investors Get Their Money Back.* His plan was extremely **clear** and **detailed**. I have to say, this **clarity** helped me decide to invest.

A plan focused on dividends can offer a realistic cash-flow scenario for investors and can be a very good option for first-time entrepreneurs. Creating a profitable company also opens the door to other exits.

<u>Selling the Company</u>

This is probably the most popular exit strategy that I have seen in my investing career. Small companies can and do get acquired by bigger companies. It's not an easy strategy by any means, but it can be **realistic** and make everyone very wealthy if the entrepreneur understands what it takes to accomplish this strategy. If this is your plan, there are a few important concepts that you must prove to your potential investors for them to jump into your company. These concepts are centered around numbers, comparisons in the industry and the skill set of the entrepreneur, all of which need to be grounded in **profit**, **realism**, **detail** and **clarity**.

First, show the potential investors that you understand that big companies don't purchase ideas, they purchase proven solutions that have demonstrable customer bases, robust profit and revenue, the promise of future growth and competitive advantage.

Companies that get sold are also companies that have audited books. If the investors sense sloppiness in your numbers, they probably will not invest. Companies that get sold have a **detailed** understanding of their profit margin and how that can be increased by a bigger company with more resources. Focusing on **profit** and showing this in your numbers will open the door to many more potential buyers, and most likely will get you a better price when you do sell the company.

One company was doing $10 million in break-even revenue at the time I invested. They subsequently grew their revenue to $100 million, yet were still spending all they made, leaving them still at break-even. They sold the company. When I invested, they were a $10 million company, and when I exited the company via a sale, they were a $100 million company.

My return? I basically got my money back after seven years.

Why do I tell you this? Because their exit strategy was correct; they sold just like they said they would. But without a focus on **profit,** it didn't do us investors much good. This is not always the case, of course, as there are plenty of examples in the dot-com boom and the more recent tech boom of companies selling for huge numbers without a **profit**. From my perspective, however, focusing your numbers on **profit** will attract more investors and provide more opportunities for a lucrative exit for both you and your investors.

Second, potential investors will be looking very closely at the comparable sales in your chosen industry. They need to believe that your company sale projections are based in **realism**. They want to see a trend of consolidation in the industry. They want to **clearly** understand why bigger companies would want to purchase your type of company rather than just create their own similar product. One company that I did invest in had a few pages in the business plan dedicated to comparable sales in their industry. They convinced me that they were indeed the type of company that gets bought and their projections were based in **reality**. I invested.

Third, most investors understand that they are investing in the entrepreneur's ability to succeed with the idea, much more than the idea itself. I will cover this point in much more detail in Chapter 9 titled *Character, Skills, Track Record and Distraction-Free*. Potential investors will be asking themselves if you, the entrepreneur, have the skill set and ability to pull off a sale of your company at the level that you are projecting. This means you have to prove not only that you have a good idea, but also that you and your team have the ability (skills, character, drive and experience) to succeed with your goal of selling your company.

If you want to speed up the money raising process, spend some extra time on the section of your business plan usually called *The Management Team*. Stand in the investor's shoes and ask yourself if you and your team have the attributes to sell your company for what you say you can. Investors want to see the background of everyone on the team. We want to see **detailed** experience that gives us confidence. If you can help investors believe in you and your team, your chances of raising money increases significantly.

As an exit strategy, selling your company can be a lucrative and exciting scenario for all shareholders. However, the plan and the team to get you there must be detailed, credible and compelling.

The Company Buying Back Its Shares

Although this is one of the ways investors can get their money back, if you are serious about raising money, I don't recommend this for your exit strategy. There are a couple of reasons why I say this. First, there is an inherent conflict of interest in this strategy. If the company wants to buy back its shares, it's usually because it's doing very well and the original founders want more of the company. Why would an investor want to sell their shares if there was something exciting around the corner or the profits were growing at an amazing pace?

Secondly, if the plan was realistic growth with a buy-back exit strategy (say, in year five), usually the ROI that the company can afford to purchase the shares back isn't high enough for an investor to justify the inherent risk involved in startup investing.

There are, however, some specific companies where I have seen this strategy work. These are companies that have reduced the risk through collateral and do not need to offer the normal startup ROI. An example of this would be a real estate play where the investors owned 70% of an apartment building with no banks involved. This sort of collateral can reduce the need for a super-high ROI and make it possible for them to get excited about being bought out at a later date.

I also believe this type of strategy can be used as a backup strategy. Assure investors that, if the original exit goal does not happen, the alternate plan stipulates that shares will start to be purchased back from investors during a specific year. Be careful how you present this backup plan, however, because you do not want to give your potential investors reason to think your first exit plan might fail.

Investor buy-back stipulations in the event of the company not being able to deliver on its primary exit strategy can help allay investor concerns, but they must be thoughtfully crafted.

Taking Your Company Public

Taking your company public is also called an Initial Public Offering (IPO). Basically, it is the sale of stock that allows the general public to buy equity in your company. The decision to take your company public is a big one that carries many variables and many new responsibilities. There are full-length books on the subject. Here, I offer some basics for you to think about and a few pros and cons that will help you understand what is involved. This can help you prepare for potential investor questions if this is the exit strategy of choice.

Pros:

1. Taking your company public is very prestigious. It signals to the world that you have "made it."
2. If done properly, it can be a great way for the founders and the shareholders to get a healthy return on their investment.
3. Going public can help attract great talent and get you in the door with many new clients, vendors, suppliers or prospective business partners.
4. An IPO is a way to generate a lot of cash that can be used for many things, such as acquiring other companies and scaling operations.
5. Taking your company public is a huge awareness boost. If you are successful, this can put you on the radar for bigger companies seeking to acquire a portion of your company at a healthy valuation.

Cons:

1. Taking your company public is extremely difficult and most potential investors (at least this investor) will not consider this exit seriously unless you have done this before or have key team members who have been successful with an IPO.
2. Taking a company public typically involves a great deal of legal work and is very expensive. You will need to take those costs into account and include them in your financial plan.
3. Even if you succeed in going public, there are huge risks. If your stock performs poorly after going public, this can hurt your business by

damaging the market's perception of your company and lessen the possibility of a nice ROI for yourself and your investors. Furthermore, in order to protect the public from insider trading, there are requirements regarding when the founders and early investors can sell their shares. Often, the stock price can do well for a while, but by the time the early investors and founders can sell their shares, the price may not be so pretty. Once you are public, the reasons for your stock price rising or falling are, at some level, out of your control, leaving you and your early investors' ROI at major risk.

4. Going public means giving up a large degree of control. Raising money for this strategy alone means huge dilution; selling shares to the public means more dilution. As the founder, going public can mean putting yourself in a vulnerable position that might jeopardize your leadership of the enterprise.

5. Being a public company is an arduous and invasive process. Public companies have strict quarterly financial reporting and procedural obligations that can be time draining at best. The SEC also requires public companies to report what was once private information. This can include data about your product or service, customers and customer contracts, salaries, bonuses or any other ways the team is incentivized. Also, directors' and officers' personal liabilities increase with the IPO strategy.

As with the other exit strategies, potential investors will need to believe whole-heartedly that you have the skill set, the ability and the team to take the company public. Most investors understand how difficult and complicated this process is; therefore, making sure your business plan is rooted in **profits, realism, detail** and **clarity** is more important than ever. To be sure, I would only recommend this strategy to very seasoned entrepreneurs, as it is by far the hardest to sell to potential investors and the most difficult to implement.

Going public can bring in massive new capital and credibility in the market, but it is a complex process with major risks, significant costs and regulatory burdens.

Summary

There is no right or wrong exit strategy. The key to raising money is really about proving that you can execute on the exit that you choose. Understanding that investors are "stuck" until you implement an exit for them is the first step. And if I have not said it enough: **Focusing on profits** is music to investors' ears. Investors must believe that your exit strategy numbers are based in **realism** or they will not invest. And please don't forget: **Detail, detail, detail**, but not at the expense of **clarity.** Confusion is not your friend.

To win over your potential investors, choose an exit strategy that addresses all these considerations.

CHAPTER 5
SAME PAGE PHILOSOPHY

I have left many a meeting with entrepreneurs who had great ideas and seemed sharp enough to succeed, but also with the nagging feeling that I was joining more of a poker game than a potential marriage. Nothing makes me run from investment opportunities faster.

Structuring your offer and your operating agreement or bylaws in such a way that proves to investors that you will get rich the same way they will get rich is paramount to raising money. Investors want you, the founder, to get wealthy — ridiculously wealthy, in fact. But they want you to get wealthy the same way they do — as a shareholder. There is a golden rule for companies that have shareholders: Maximize shareholder wealth. It's so obvious that it's easy to overlook; it should be used as a filter as you make the decisions that will grow your company.

As covered in the previous section, shareholders only have four ways to get wealthy: Dividends, sale of the company, company buyback of investor shares or going public.

I want to share with you some principles that will help investors not just *hope* that you are on the same page with them, but *know in their gut* that you are on the same page. These simple little ideas will ensure that you and the investors are entering more of a marriage than a poker game. I call these the Uncle Bob Test, the Salary Cap Test, and the Democracy Test. They are basic indicators that show investors, for certain, that you want and need the exit strategy to be a success as quickly as they do.

Prove that to them, and watch "maybe" investors turn into "yes" investors.

Uncle Bob Test

I was 99.9% ready to invest in a startup that had been pitched to me. This was going to be my third or fourth investment, so I was still fairly new to the game. Everything about the investment sounded perfect. He was a sharp guy who knew his stuff. I understood the business model and was convinced that this was going to be my next investment. Then I asked the question, the answer to which caused me to second-guess and eventually decline the opportunity.

I asked him who else had invested in his idea. Then I asked him if he had tried to raise money from his close friends and family. His answer was what gave birth to the Uncle Bob Test. He basically said that he did not want his friends and family in the business because he didn't want any "weirdness" down the road.

At the time, this sort of made sense, as bringing family into a risky business could make holiday dinners a bit awkward. But the more I pondered this fact, the more it bothered me. How would making your family and friends a great return on their money make things awkward? Clearly, this entrepreneur thought that there was a decent chance that this thing would go bad.

This may sound like a contradiction on my part, because earlier I mentioned that we investors must plan on many of our startup investments going bad. Statistically, 9 out of 10 startups fail, necessitating a huge potential ROI because our winners are going to have to make up for our losers. The bottom line is this: Starting a company and wildly succeeding is one of the hardest things on Earth to accomplish. It takes a special and resilient kind of person who just absolutely refuses to fail. It takes someone so dedicated to success that they will go the extra mile and the extra hundred miles after.

Succeeding with a startup takes someone who believes without a doubt that they will succeed. Your family and friends (your Uncle Bob) would be the first people you would want to bring in if you truly believe that you can execute your vision successfully. As an investor, this is what I am looking for: Someone who knows they are going to wildly succeed.

The Uncle Bob Test is about having skin in the game. Investors are not just looking at the idea, but looking to see what relationships the entrepreneur is willing to risk. Having your own hard-earned money in the deal is also very important. I probably would not invest if the entrepreneur did not have any of his money at risk. Having your friends and family, however, signals an even higher level of confidence and commitment. Losing your own money is one thing; losing your friends' and family's money is something quite different. This might sound intense, but it absolutely puts you on the same page as your investors — wanting and almost needing that exit strategy to happen sooner than later.

The caveat here is that I am not encouraging unrealistic guarantees to anyone, much less your friends and family. They also need to know that investing is risky, and that there is a potential of losing all their money. The point, again, if I have not driven it home yet, is that bringing friends and family into the game speaks directly to the level of the entrepreneur's belief.

One further word on this concept: The Uncle Bob Test speaks directly to the fear of failure, a hurdle that, for some entrepreneurs, is paralyzing. This is a big concept, beyond the scope of this book, and more appropriately addressed in a consulting format. There are other ways for an entrepreneur to demonstrate their level of belief, but again, that is why this is more an art and than a science.

Passing the Uncle Bob Test signals to investors the level of seriousness with which you're approaching success, and helps money-raising happen faster.

Salary Cap Test

I learned this one the hard way. One of my early investments was going south while all of us shareholders watched the CEO put $200K per year into his pocket. It took about two and a half years for the company to finally fail. Our CEO made half a million dollars over that time while we lost every dime we put in. He justified this with the argument that the $200K is what he could have made at another job if he was not running this company. While that has some level of validity, it certainly did not put him on the same page as the investors.

Think about it this way: That CEO might be worth $200K per year for what he did, but he was not "getting wealthy" the same way we investors were going to get wealthy — dividends, sale of the company or an IPO. That CEO didn't need the exit strategy to pan out. We were fatally misaligned.

Let's address some of the common objections around this issue, some of which you may have now. Does this mean that founders have to be poor until they exit? What if our personal expenses are $200K per year? Certainly you need to be able to cover your personal expenses while you slave night and day to make the company a success. Sometimes it takes big salaries to attract the talent needed to take things to the next level. Isn't top talent a consideration?

Remember, the point of putting yourself on a salary cap is to demonstrate to your investors that you are on the same page as them, that you're as committed to the successful exit as they are. That you will get wealthy — even wildly wealthy — but it will happen the same way the investors get wealthy. Keeping that in mind, there are ways to incentivize and even put money in your pockets without breaking the Same Page Rule.

One of the best ways to incentivize yourself and your key people is with stock options. Basing your stock option agreement on a mixture of time and production goals puts you on the same page with investors, and hitting your goals can put a huge amount of money in your pocket. This does not solve the personal cash flow issues, but keeping your personal expenses to a minimum in the first few years of your company definitely sends the right signal to your investors.

Besides stock options, another incentive that directly addresses the cash-flow concern is using bonuses based on growth and profit. Nothing puts the driver of the business and the shareholders on the same page better than this. In a very tangible way, this causes the driver of the business to want (almost need) profits and want those profits to grow each year, which is exactly what the investor wants. There are numerous ways of setting up bonus plans for multiple key people. I have even seen them used for the entire team. Bonus plans work and can be set up on a quarterly or yearly basis.

Commissions are my absolute favorite incentive because they address cash flow *and* demonstrate a willingness to get in the sales trenches. I absolutely believe that one of the best things that the founder can do with 10 to 15 hours a week is to sell. The objection that I usually hear to this is, "I don't have time with all the other things on my plate," or "I am not cut out for sales." All of that might be true, however, this solution is something that does wonders for your business and your investors. First, it keeps you on the front line for part of your day, giving you real insight to the many customer and market challenges that you wouldn't see if you were always in the back office. Second, your team will respect your willingness to get out there and swing the bat with the sales people. Third, you will be surprised at how well you do, even if you don't think of yourself as a salesperson. That business card that says Founder, President or CEO will help open doors — plus you know the product or service better than anyone. You also want to succeed more than anyone. Investors will love this. Showing them that you are not only running the show but getting out there and making sales happen will earn their respect and confidence. And fourth, it will help you in the Lean Org Chart Test, which I cover later.

My belief is that good salespeople should be the best-paid folks in the company; so, if the commission structure is set up properly, this plan will definitely help solve your personal cash flow issues.

The important thing to remember when structuring any type of incentive plan is that they need to work for everyone involved — including the investors. They need to truly incentivize the person on the plan, and at the same time, be in line with the imperative to maximize shareholder wealth. Do this, and you show investors that you are on the same page with them. Once you're on the same page, the more likely money gets raised.

Entrepreneurial teams that can forego fat salaries and tie their rewards to agreed-upon performance milestones can win investor confidence and funding.

Democracy Test

This test is probably the hardest one to swallow and most definitely the most misunderstood. It's about control of the company. It's about your willingness to allow big company decisions to be shared by others. It's about understanding the concept, "too close to the trees to see the forest." As harsh as this might sound, it's about moving from a dictatorship to a democracy. Let me explain.

As I mentioned earlier, we investors are usually stepping into a position of vulnerability. We are giving up control of our money. We are becoming minority shareholders of a non-marketable security.

Now for the tough part: For us investors to be on the same page as you, the entrepreneur, you would also have to be willing to give up total control of the decision-making. What does this mean? It means that you would have to be willing for the founders to collectively move below the 50% equity mark.

As I write, I know the objections that are brewing in your mind. You probably have been coached by many people to "never give up control of your company." I understand this, and I would agree — if you are talking about giving up control to one group or one investor. Then the Same Page Philosophy is violated in the reverse. I would be equally concerned if one investor or one group of investors is in control of the company and calling all the shots. This is not what I am talking about. I am talking about a democracy with a healthy mix of employee shares, different groups of investor shares and founder shares all owning less than 50%, therefore bringing about real, thoughtful debate over the big decisions that the company will be facing in the future.

Another objection might be: "What about second and third rounds of money-raising? As founders, if we give up control too early, we might end up with such a small piece of the pie that it's not even worth the hard work." I get this. This is a very real and valid concern. If second and third rounds of funding are planned, you should have an idea of future valuation based on projected profit/revenue that will help all of us do the math and figure out where the founding team will end up. The end equity scenario after the money raising is what we investors are looking at. Will this end up a democracy or not?

Example:
Two rounds of fundraising are planned. First-round investors purchase 40% of the company leaving 60% for founders and employees. Second-round investors purchase 20% of the company at a higher valuation, leaving the first-round investors diluted to 32% and the founders and employees diluted to 48%. After the second round, the three groups create a voting democracy with no single group holding enough shares to overpower the other two.

During the interim between the first and second rounds there are ways to give up your 60% veto power. One way is to have some of that 60% on the books as non-voting shares. This would keep the financial interest of 60% intact, while giving up some control regarding the voting shares. Another way to create a democracy with regards specific items such as salary decisions, dividend decisions, etc. is to establish certain decisions that would require a super majority vote (say 67%) to pass.

This is a frequent area of discussion with many of my consulting clients, since specific concerns can arise quickly. But for the purposes of this document, the goal is to demonstrate the importance of preserving a voting democracy.

A third objection might be: "If as the founders we only end up owning X% of the company, it's not worth all the hard work." Whenever I hear this objection, I usually tell my Warren Buffett story. I have asked many an entrepreneur what percentage, one of the richest men in the world, Warren Buffett owns in his company Berkshire Hathaway?' To make the point, please stop reading and put a number in your head. What do you think? 50%, 40%, 30%? Although he maintains 30.71% of the voting shares, the actual economic stake Warren Buffett owns, as of 2020, is 16.45%. He is a great example of the concept "less is more." All of us, including investors, can get hung up on what percentage of the company we own. This is unfortunate, as I believe, it's being concerned about the wrong thing. What matters is the ROI, both for the investors' money and for the founders' money, time and energy. I have specific winner investments where I paid $25K for 20% of the company, and one where I invested $100K, which bought less than 2%. Both made the founders and the investors a lot of money. Both followed the Same Page Philosophy, where neither the founders nor any one group of investors had control of the company. You don't always need a large percentage to make a large amount of money.

Remember the point of this chapter: *Same Page Philosophy.* With this in mind, there are many ways to structure your equity plan in which this idea is protected and used to attract investors.

For example, with a C-Corp, you can have voting shares and non-voting shares built into the bylaws. You can also have dilutable shares and non-dilutable shares if need be. With LLCs you can use the super majority concept to fulfill the Democracy Test, meaning it would take a super majority (say 67%) to change or make specific decisions that are important to investors, like dividends or salaries. Using these and other tools to assure the original investors that the end goal is democracy will go a long way in raising money.

It's the control that is the important part to think about, not the equity stake. I am working with a client right now where we are devising a plan to split the founder's shares into voting shares and non-voting shares. He might end up owning more than 50% of the company, even after all the money-raising, because his ROI numbers are great for investors. However, he is willing to reduce his personal voting shares to less than 50%. Because of this, I most likely will invest.

Being willing to give up control while also making sure one investment group doesn't take control is a big part of protecting the Same Page Philosophy. Protecting this philosophy can dramatically help you raise money and, more importantly, help you wildly succeed.

Proof is in the Operating Agreement or Bylaws

Regarding the Same Page Philosophy, I stated early in this chapter: *Prove that to investors, and watch "maybe" investors turn into "yes" investors.* I thought I should add a few thoughts surrounding this statement.

What you want to prove is that you are in the same boat with the investors; that you need/want the exit strategy as much as the investors do. This means demonstrating that you are living the Same Page Philosophy in everything you do surrounding your business. Some of these things like the *Uncle Bob Test* are evident in your cap table. Other things, like the *Salary Cap Test*, the *Democracy Test* or even the *Board of Directors Test* (which I will discuss in the next chapter) would be best if they were committed inside the Operating Agreement or Bylaws.

For clarity, I should mention that an Operating Agreement and Bylaws are essentially the same thing. Both are the official documents that govern the rules, provisions and decision powers of the company. Operating Agreements are typically used with LLCs and Partnerships, and are signed by all the members, and Bylaws are used with most S-corps and C-corps and signed by their board of directors.

Saying you are willing to have a salary cap or saying that you are committed to democracy voting is one thing. Committing yourself in the Operating Agreement or Bylaws is quite a step above. I highly suggest that you commit to these things in writing in your Operating Agreement or Bylaws. It's like handcuffing yourself to the investor – now it's guaranteed that everyone wins or loses together.

Most Operating Agreements or Bylaws are written by attorneys, and won't naturally include these sorts of promises. But don't let that hold you back. It can be as simple as adding a section called "Miscellaneous Provisions" and listing your promises, like salary caps, board seat intentions, future option pool commitments, future cap table goals, etc. Of course, you would want to check with your attorney, but don't let them talk you out of this sort of thing. Remember, your goal is to maximize shareholders' wealth; your attorneys' goal is to protect you. There shouldn't be a conflict here, but you will need to hold your ground.

The Same Page Philosophy is a good thing when verbalized; it's a great thing when cemented in writing! By doing so, not only do I believe your venture will have a better chance of success, you have also turned your Operating Agreement into an awesome sales tool for raising money. Showing investors that you walk your talk will move many of those "maybe" investors to "yes" investors!

The Operating Agreement/Bylaws are great places to commit in writing promises that will prove to your investors that you truly believe in the Same Page Philosophy. When done correctly and honestly, these documents now become a tool, helping you raise money!

CHAPTER 6
ORGANIZATIONAL CHART

This chapter is about ultimate responsibility: Where the buck stops. It's also about trimming the fat in your organizational chart and still knowing when two heads are better than one. It's about appointing and respecting a board of directors. And it's about structure.

Investors look closely at these things because they know that an unorganized team has very little chance of succeeding. They want to know who is responsible for what, and who, ultimately, is in the driver's seat. Managers managing managers is also a red flag for investors. They want to see a lean team, with everybody filling essential roles. They want to know how the decision making flows through the company, because good and timely decisions are the essence of success. They also want to see a respectable board of directors and understand what decisions will end up needing a vote from that board.

One Driver Test

If you have read anything else I've written on this topic, you might be familiar with the story where I turned down an investment opportunity, giving rise to what I call The One Driver Test. I'll summarize the story, as it will help make the point clear.

It was going to be my 17th investment. I was being pitched by two guys who, in my opinion, had what it took to succeed. I totally understood the industry they were entering and had connections that would have helped. They had their own skin in the game, and they had friends and family in the deal. It was the perfect investment, except for one thing: I knew the two were good friends and I wanted to see who was ultimately responsible for the business. I asked to look at the organizational chart, wanting to see who reported to whom. The answer caused me to walk from this opportunity. They said they were both equally responsible. They were both at the top of the org chart. They assured me that they had different roles and that they were both committed to working crazy hours, if need be, to make sure the business was a success.

At first this sounded like a great answer to the question. Two heads are better than one, right? To be sure, I have learned the importance of the One Driver Test through experience; experience that cost me a lot of money. When it comes to brainstorming, advising, guiding and other important pieces of the puzzle, I agree that two heads (even three or four) are better than one. This can be seen in a solid and experienced board of directors, which I will discuss later in this chapter. However, taking a company from a business plan to a wild success is so difficult, so time consuming and so frustrating that it requires accepting what looks like a paradox on the surface. It takes a team to succeed, but it also requires one and only one ultimate leader. Let me unpack this concept for you.

Look at a company scenario with two leaders — two equal equity partners with equal responsibilities. What happens when one of them falls in love, gets married or has a baby? What happens when one of them decides that work/life balance is more important than it once was? What happens if one of them has more friends or family in the deal then the other? What happens if the team begins to gravitate toward and favor one of the leaders over the other?

The point is that two equal leaders is a recipe for conflict. Conflict, at this level, is a recipe for failure. Sure, it's possible that one of the potential issues I mentioned above gets ironed out and one leader takes on the driver role. But even given this, there is the "fairness" question that will be left unresolved. Why should I work harder than you when we both own the same amount of equity? Why should you get all the credit as the leader when we started this together? Divorce, at any level, can cause unexpected ugliness. In my experience, having one and only one ultimate driver should be an important part of your organizational chart if you are going to raise money.

Although it takes a team to wildly succeed, and the team is filled with many leaders with much responsibility, investors and the board need to see one person, and one person only, step up and take ultimate responsibility for CEO-level decisions. Demonstrating this in the organizational chart will help you raise money.

<u>Lean Org Chart Test</u>

I look at a lot of organizational charts. Although I have been a sales manager in my past and understand the need for managers, in the beginning stages of a company, having too many managers is a red flag. It tells me that too many of the founding team want to be executives too early. It wastes precious startup money. This may sound a bit harsh, but let me help you understand the mind of the investor with regards to what I call the Lean Org Chart Test. Investors know from experience that things take twice as long to finish and cost twice as much as the original plan. They just do. That's why investors will be looking closely at the role of each team member.

We want to see that everyone taking a salary has a role that is absolutely imperative, and no one is avoiding the hard work. Two sales people do not need a sales manager. Two tech guys do not need an extra third person hired to oversee them. A good rule of thumb is everyone involved in the beginning stages should be doing work that is directly connected to either making money or saving money.

In the first stages of the company, here is the way most investors think: The role of an executive *is* the nitty gritty. It is doing sales. It is learning QuickBooks. It is getting deeply involved with the technologies of the company. It is everything that needs doing. It is the hard work.

Moving out of these roles at the correct time is equally important and absolutely necessary to scale, but avoiding these types of tasks too early is a red flag to investors.

Please don't think this test is just about not burning unnecessary money. It is also about developing your skills and understanding of every aspect of your business. Any time you can truly stand in the shoes of all your employees and feel the pain they feel, it helps you as a leader, it deepens your skill set and it most definitely wins the respect of investors.

Startups are not the right place for layers of management; every role on the team must be critical and fully engaged in proving the model and becoming profitable. Before you go in front of an investor, you should have an invincible argument for every spot on your org chart and demonstrate your willingness to do the hard work.

Board of Directors Test
Creating and respecting a board of directors is one of the cornerstones that shows investors that you understand

what you are getting into by raising money. Most solely owned small businesses do not have a board of directors simply because they don't really need one. When a business is owned by one person (or maybe a husband and a wife), there is no real need to create such a formal chain of command. Decisions get made over dinner or coffee, and the only people who are affected by these decisions are the owners. Once you bring investors into your business, all this changes. Now, like it or not, you have a fiduciary responsibility to maximize the new shareholders' wealth. As a sole owner, you could make your salary anything you wanted it to be or spend your excess cash on business items that you also used for personal reasons. You could make just about any decision you wanted and the only "person" you had to worry about would be the IRS. Bringing in investors adds not only complexity to your business dynamics, but also a tremendous responsibility.

The board of directors, if looked at properly, is your friend. It's easy for entrepreneurs to find themselves "too close to the forest to see the trees." Since the board is not caught up in the day-to-day operations, they can lend an invaluable bird's-eye perspective to decision making.

Traditionally, the board gives the entrepreneur boundaries regarding decisions. Day-to-day decisions are made without consulting the board, but major things such as opening a new location, taking out a loan or deciding on whether to pay a dividend are voted on by the board of directors. When the entrepreneur has a big idea that they would like to implement, the board of directors ensures that a formal process is now followed. Rather than just making these decisions solo, the entrepreneur must now be more deliberate, selling their ideas to the board.

This may sound burdensome, but it's really a beautiful thing. By having to take the time and put together a presentation on why this or that is a good idea, it helps make sure the decision up for a vote is thoroughly examined. Yes, some ideas will get shot down, but the ones that pass the vote of the board are much more likely to be successful. The board of directors serves you by keeping you accountable for your ideas and decisions — and helping protect you from the potentially bad ones.

Usually, the board of directors is made up of people who have invested a sizable amount of money in your company. Sometimes the board of directors also contains non-shareholders who have experience in the industry. Both are good strategies, but it's important that everyone on the board is incentivized as shareholders so the company's decisions reflect the primary imperative: Maximize shareholder wealth.

For board members who already have a sizable portion of the company, there usually does not need to be any sort of compensation for their role on the board. For outsiders without equity, in my view, stock options or profit sharing should be used to incentivize them for their work on the board, rather than fee-based compensation. This method of incentivizing stays true to the Same Page Philosophy discussed earlier.

Keep in mind that the board should also have authority to replace the founding CEO if needed. Founding the company vs. scaling the company are two different skill sets. Since the success of the company is everyone's goal, this is sometimes the prudent and the best decision for all shareholders.

My advice is to start with a small board of directors — meaning you plus two others. A three-person board is a great starting point because it keeps the process efficient, and adding to the board later is much easier than the other way around. If you want more minds to help guide you or more mentors that you feel the need to include, you can also have what's called a board of advisors to go alongside your board of directors — the difference being that the advisors don't have a vote. It's a way to open the door for more advice and input without slowing down the voting and meeting process. *Advisors* can be great, but most investors will still be looking for a proper board of *directors*, either planned or already in place.

A board of directors shows investors that you're serious about growth and making the best decisions possible. Pick them wisely and you'll have a better shot at success.

CHAPTER 7
EMPLOYEE OPTION POOL

In my early 20s, I learned a concept from a man named Mort Utley. He said, "help enough other people get what they want, and you will get what you want." It took me a while and a few hard lessons for me to understand how this applies to the startup world, but that is the way truth works. True concepts typically apply to many areas of life.

Companies that generously share the equity with not just the executives, but with all levels of employees tend to very well. There is of course much debate and controversy surrounding this concept, as sometimes these things can be more for 'show' than actually benefit the worker. That said, setting aside a portion of your company for future employees must be credible, meaningful and generous for it make a difference long term. Nothing feels better than seeing people that help make your company succeed get rewarded in a powerful way.

In this chapter, I would like to give you the what, why and how of employee option pools, including anecdotes from my personal experience that should underline the points in your mind. By applying these ideas, you can not only strengthen your case to a prospective investor, but also lay the groundwork for an incentive plan that drives your team in enthusiastic unison toward all your goals.

Employee option pools are a topic that quickly exceeds the scope of this chapter. Many great minds have covered the in-depth technical aspects of employee option pools, so understand that this is an overview of the concept as it applies to raising capital and the mind of the investor. Consult with a qualified attorney before structuring an employee option pool.

What is an Employee Option Pool?

An employee option pool is the amount of equity that has been set aside as an incentive program for employees. There is also a strategy called profit sharing that is similar to an option pool, in which employees enjoy a portion of the profits, but don't actually ever own the equity. I personally prefer the option pool over profit sharing, and I will explain the advantages later in this chapter.

From my perspective, option pools should represent at least 20% of the company's equity. Every company is different, so this is only a rule of thumb, but the point is that it needs to be significant if it's going to have any real meaning. Option pools can be set up for LLCs, S-corps or C-corps, and offer equity with different privileges than that purchased by investors. While employee option pools reduce the entrepreneur's percentage in the company, they can have a big upside when it comes to your long-term wealth and success.

Why Choose to Set Up an Employee Option Pool?

One of my earlier investments was in a copy machine company. When I initially invested, the economy was in a boom and it seemed that this opportunity couldn't fail. The entrepreneur had a CFO background. He was a natural numbers guy, watching over the costs, the margins and the cash flow, all of which we investors love to see.

He did not have an employee option pool, and at the time, none of us investors really thought too much about it. The employees had great packages, including solid salaries and health insurance. The sales guys were making great money through commissions and everyone enjoyed year-end bonuses that made Christmas shopping fun!

The entrepreneur ran a tight ship and things went very well with our investment for years. Then 2008 rolled around and things started to unravel. The company was actually set up to weather the economy, as it had many of its clients on service contracts that kept revenue coming in. The problem ended up being the revolving door through which the sales team and other key employees were continually passing in and out. Not being able to keep top-notch salespeople and not being able to keep other key team players during the hard times set the company back at least five years. It was painful to watch. It was even more painful to see our financial investment suffer unnecessarily.

Why did these top team members leave the company? As I see it, they left because they saw themselves as employees rather than owners. As employees, they had no real reason to stick out the hard times. There was no incentive to stay around. Their upside consisted of base salaries, commissions, end-of-year bonuses and health insurance. When commissions and bonuses took a hit, there was little reason not to shop around for other job offers. Would a stake in the company, through stock options, have incentivized them to help the company weather the downturn? My experience says that it would have.

It seemed that almost every company was struggling in the years between 2008 and 2012. Those were tough times. Yet, another company in which I am currently invested managed to keep their entire team intact through the struggles. They got more efficient; they worked as a team and thought outside the box. They worked smarter, emerging stronger than before. How did this company keep its key members through the storm? They were all shareholders or were earning options to become shareholders. They were like family. They took pay cuts and pay delays together. They thought long-term rather than short-term. As shareholders or soon-to-be shareholders, they believed that helping the company improve through adversity would be more rewarding than trying to find another job.

The point is this: It takes a team to build a startup from nothing to something great. One person, regardless of how smart or dynamic, cannot build something huge. Option pools, when set up correctly, help create that team. They create owners, and by extension, a "We" company culture. It gives people a reason to work late, be problem solvers instead of problem finders, and soldier through tough times. This kind of loyalty gives the company a winning edge. And investors love to invest in companies with a winning edge.

I mentioned profit sharing as an alternative to stock options earlier in this chapter. Profit sharing is similar in that the employees share in the profits, but they do not actually own shares in the company. I prefer stock options to profit sharing for two major reasons: Profit sharing doesn't have the same emotional and loyalty-building value. Also, stock options have an added potential lump sum payment value in case the exit is selling the company. Emotionally, profit sharing feels more like a bonus plan then ownership. If the exit plan is strictly dividends, this strategy can work, but if there is a chance of selling the company, a profit sharing agreement will never be as effective.

Another reason to create an option pool and help your employees build wealth is the satisfaction of helping others achieve their financial goals. You're more than someone who just cuts the paychecks; you're a leader that encourages everyone around them to find the best in themselves. You have created a business that truly rewards the everyday sweat and toil that goes into building a company.

I believe the saying I learned as a young adult holds true for the startup world: "If you help enough people get what they want, you get what you want."

Employee option pools, if set up correctly, can incentivize better performance and give the company a better chance of enriching all shareholders. Offering employees a chance to become shareholders is a wise long-term strategy.

How to Create and Implement an Employee Option Pool

There are two aspects to a successful employee option pool. The first is creating the option pool: Deciding on what percentage to set aside and the nuts and bolts of actually setting it aside. The second is implementing the option pool — deciding who gets how much equity, how they vest into the equity and if they get to keep it when and if they leave the company.

Creating the Option Pool

The nuts and bolts of creating an option pool are a bit different with C-corps then with LLCs or S-corps, however, the end results are incredibly similar. With C-corps, the options are literally 'set aside' and owned by no specific person. The pool usually consists of authorized shares which get issued (thus diluting current shareholders) as the employees and others with options purchase them. With LLCs and S-corps, all equity must be owned by a taxpaying entity or person because of the flow through tax code. Therefore, the 'setting aside' is done through a commitment in the Operating Agreement for everyone (or sometimes just the founders) to be willing to sell and be gradually diluted as equity is purchased by the option holders.

This is a frequent topic we address with our consulting clients, but it is still a good idea to have an attorney help you navigate the technicalities of implementation.

The important part of creating the option pool is not the technicalities, but deciding on the amount that you are setting aside and the terms of how employees can acquire that portion. I said earlier that I like to see 20% or more of the company set aside, but let me better explain myself. The point of the option pool is to create real incentive for the key employees to stick around and build the company through the hard times, for the long haul.

People, especially key people, are not stupid. They will do the math and figure out what their stock represents on a percentage basis. They will calculate into the future how much the company will be worth and, therefore, how much their percentage will be worth once they are fully vested. They will ask themselves if dividends will be the way their equity will turn into retirement — or will it be the sale of the company? They will make their decision to leave or stay based on math, estimated valuation of the company, and belief in your projections.

There is no "magic percentage" that makes an option pool work. The magic is offering something enticing, but also attainable. Does this sound familiar? Your key team members, who you want to stick around and who will be given stock options for doing so, will be thinking much like investors. So, the work you must do is similar to when you came up with your initial valuation. You need to stand in the shoes of your key people and offer them something that's both exciting and realistic — exciting and realistic enough for them to stick around through the stress and uncertainty of building a brand new venture. Exciting and realistic enough to make all other offers that they will be getting not worth following. And like coming up with a proper valuation, this too is definitely more of an art than a science.

Similar to your valuation work, the best way to start is with your key team members. How much money in the form of dividends, or by selling the company, will motivate your key people to stick around for five, seven, or ten years? Figure out a motivation dollar value for each of them. After you know those numbers, work backward to see what percentage of the company that dollar figure represents or will represent with your realistic pro forma. From that percentage, you can break that out into shares or equity percentage per employee.

There is a strategy of giving everyone stock options regardless of how important their role, which, although not necessary, I think is fantastic. The amount needed to motivate each of your general employees is obviously not as large as your key people, but it still needs to be exciting and realistic enough to help create loyalty, enthusiasm and inspiration for your new enterprise.

While there are multiple ways to successfully structure an option pool, it must appropriately incentivize your key people, thus creating an "owner" mindset versus an "employee" mindset.

Implementation of the Option Pool

Implementing the employee option pool has many moving parts. It's difficult to provide an exact formula for an effective option pool. Every business has its unique concerns. But here is a helpful list of considerations that can shape your thinking as you solve the puzzle:

1. Everyone is motivated differently. As much as I believe in employee option pools, there are some people out there that are just not motivated by stock or equity. It's important that you have the conversations with your potential team members and find out what their value levers are.

2. Everyone's view of a retirement nest egg is different. A person's age and their marital status are both factors to consider. Some people would be very excited to see their stock turn into $300K after 10 years. Others will need to see themselves becoming millionaires over a five- or seven-year commitment.

3. Sometimes it's best to have your key people write a check to "buy in" and have their options based on their initial investment, plus time. Other

times this is not possible, and it is only time that earns the options.

4. Basing options on time alone is not always best. Adding production goals to the option agreement can really boost productivity.

5. The price of the options is a real factor. Does their pay give them enough extra money to be able to take advantage of the options? Does the discount in share price motivate them enough to take advantage of the options?

6. The shares or equity purchased through options can be set up so that the buyer can keep them for life even if they leave the company or set up where, if they leave the company, they have to sell the shares back to the company at a formulated market price with some sort of buy out schedule over a specific amount of years. The latter way of structuring options helps keep the option pool alive and rotating through new employees but is typically less motivating to the ones with the options.

7. Understanding the "golden handcuff" concept can help you set up the vesting correctly. For example, if one of your employees has options to purchase 10,000 shares of the company, they shouldn't have the option to purchase 1,429 shares each year for seven years. The best way to set up the vesting schedule is on a graduating scale. For example, the first year they have the option to purchase 250 shares, the second year

500 shares, the third year 750 shares, the fourth year 1,250 shares, the fifth year 1,750 shares, the sixth year 2,250 shares and the final year 3,250 shares. The total is the 10,000 shares you promised, but the incentive to stay the full seven years is maximized.

Implementing your employee stock option pool can seem complicated, but it's rooted in common sense. Stand in the shoes of the people you want to have stick around for the long haul. Then create a realistic and exciting plan that will keep them on board and motivated with an "owner" mindset. Keep it that simple and let an attorney help you turn your option plan into a legal agreement.

Chapter 8
Raising Money is Selling

Entrepreneurs love their idea — as they should! However, this love sometimes causes them to think their idea will sell itself. Unfortunately, "build it and they will come" rarely works for getting a product or service to market, and most definitely won't work when it comes to raising money. When it comes to raising money, like it or not, selling is your job. There are thousands of books written on the topic of selling, so for the purpose of this book, I will highlight some selling points that will specifically help you raise money.

1. Always stay extremely excited about your idea, as passion is one of the most contagious human traits, but never show any sort of desperation for needing money. Desperation causes people to run the other way.

2. Invite tough questions. Don't allow yourself to be rattled by direct and personal questions. Also,

don't forget to ask questions, too. This will help you gauge investor interest level along the way while avoiding a monologue. Questions both ways keep the pitch alive and healthy.

3. Never leave a meeting without setting up another meeting. Investing is usually a decision that is made over several meetings. It takes some courting on your part, and one easy sale that you should always make is selling the potential investor to meet again at a later date. Get it in the calendar before you say goodbyes.

4. Be teachable. Ask yourself what you did right and wrong on the last pitch. Ask your partners, who were in the room with you, what they thought. Even investors who have said "no" can teach you a lot if you are willing to learn. Just say something like, "I really want to learn how investors think so I can adjust and improve my offering, so if you wouldn't mind, can you give me a few of the reasons you turned down the opportunity? And I am certainly open to any tips you might have, as well." You will be surprised how many people will be glad to give you their thoughts.

5. Control the controllables. Getting a "yes" is uncontrollable. Yet there are many things you can control that will increase the odds of that "yes":

- Make a prospect list.
- Call on a specific number of people every day.

- Have an accountability coach or team member to keep you on track.
- Use a system such as Salesforce.com to keep track of your leads.
- Make sure and follow up properly with every prospect.

These things are controllable. Treat this like a real sales job, do the little things and you will have a much greater chance of success.

6. Be an open book with everything you can think of with your potential investors: Personal and or company debts, hires, leases, bad press, online critics, competition, personal obligations, lawsuits, personal credit, personal life situations, equity splits (including your personal shares) and anything else you can think of. This is not a poker game. This is a marriage, and hiding things will come back to hurt you in the end. Confidence mixed with genuine humility is important. Even sharing areas of weakness can be a good thing if you explain your plan to account for them.

7. First impressions are very important. Dress sharp, but casual. An overdone look is suspicious, but sloppiness is also a turnoff. And don't forget to pick up the tab for the meeting. It's a small gesture that speaks volumes.

8. Your presentation can be on a tablet or laptop, but physical handouts are still a good idea. It

gives investors something to show their spouses or discuss with a trusted mentor. It's something that can help keep the investment opportunity front-of-mind. Make sure the handouts show them the things they are looking for. What piece of the company does their money buy? How do they get their money back? Sloppy handouts or unclear messaging about the potential investment will not help your cause.

9. Ask for referrals. Investors like to invest with friends. If you get an investor on board, it's likely you will get a few of their connections.

10. Flattery does help. Most normal people like compliments. Investors are normal people too. Letting them know that you couldn't do it without them just plain helps. It shows true humility and gratitude for people jumping in with real money and trusting you to live by the golden business rule: Maximize shareholder wealth.

Like it or not, raising money is a sales job. Regardless of your personality, if you control the controllables and follow some basic rules of selling, you will likely succeed.

CHAPTER 9

CHARACTER, SKILLS, TRACK RECORD AND DISTRACTION-FREE

I saved this chapter for the end because it's the one idea that has nothing to do with structuring your offer, exit or business plan. Yet it's critical to making all the above work, because this chapter is about you, the entrepreneur. From the perspective of the investor, the contents of this chapter are by far the most important piece to the puzzle. If you want to raise money, demonstrating to investors that you have solid character, the necessary skills, a track record of success and that you are free from distractions is an absolute prerequisite.

<u>Character and Skills</u>

Let me share one of my all-time favorite stories in my startup career. I call it the Mike Story and share it as often as I can with people. It was my second investment with Mike Hummell and because the first one went well, I had brought many friends and family into this second investment. One of those investors was my little sister Amy, who at the time was in her 20s, just out of college with her new job as a 2nd grade teacher (in other words, she was still broke). I was newly married at the time and was out of the country on an extensive traveling adventure – backpack style for 16 months – and therefore off the grid and not accessible at the time.

Amy, fresh out of college, with a low paying first teacher job started second guessing the wisdom of investing her precious $1,000 (yes, that's not a typo – one thousand dollars). She got a hold of Mike and asked if she could pull out of the investment – if he would be so kind as to buy her out and return her money.

Mike was kind... so kind that twenty years later telling the story still triggers huge emotion. He sent Amy her $1,000 and told her that she still owned her stock. He explained that this was a loan back to her and that she could pay him back another time with no interest and no time frame. About a year later, Amy received a check for $64,000 from the sale of the company.

Mike was working on the sale of the company when Amy requested him to buy her out. Honestly, I don't know many people that would have done what Mike did for my sister. It's over the top.

He could have been "kind" and had the company buy her shares back as Amy requested which would have been the most beneficial to him as the largest shareholder. Or with a little legal work, he could have probably gotten his board to approve him personally buying her shares back and pocketing the full $64K himself.

Mike however is the kind of guy that gets excited about making his investors money, even the little investors. He loves having people in the boat with him and literally gets joy out of making people a great return. I have witnessed him giving his attorney and other people huge bonuses as gifts. Who does this sort of thing? Mike does.

The challenge for investors is that it's very hard to know what kind of person we are investing in. It's my belief that only the Great Spirit knows the true heart and character of people. Certainly, investors don't need someone as generous as Mike to make good money, but we still need to determine the real (or not so real) desire of the entrepreneur to make money for us investors. I have a saying from my experience that has proven to be very true: *If the entrepreneur doesn't WANT to make investors lots of money, we most certainly will not.*

Character is difficult to "sell." My recommendation is to be authentic. Authenticity will do wonders helping us investors discover who you really are. Bragging about how "good" a person you are will not help your cause. The most important thing you can do is genuinely be You. Of course, share your experiences and personal stories if you think it will help. Don't hesitate to share mistakes as well – you're human, all of us make mistakes, but not all of us learn from them. If you have previous investors or employees who know you in this leadership role, by all means share those people as references.

Grit. Absolute determination. Someone who just won't ever quit. Super human persistence. This type of person is a prerequisite for success in the startup world. The years from starting a company to an exit are filled with justifiable reasons to give up. Problems, real problems, will show up constantly and we investors know this all too well. We are looking for someone who enjoys solving problems – someone who benefits from the negative feedback from customers, employees, investors – someone who actually wants to know the problems, so they can constantly improve.

If this sounds like you, then you're on the right path. Share your stories, share your previous struggles and how you got through them. Help us investors feel confident that we are getting to know a founder with this sort of determination.

Finally, as a reminder from the Same Page Philosophy, walking your talk goes a long way. Legally, through the Operating Agreement or Bylaws, place yourself in the same boat with us investors and raise money fast!

Proving your skill set is a little more straight forward. Part of this is a repeat from previous chapters, but it's worth another reminder: It takes a team to build a great company. It takes a leader to build a great team. We need to understand your personal strengths and your personal weaknesses. We don't need to believe you have every skill it takes to build a company; however, we need to believe you can recruit, motivate and build a successful team – on a shoestring budget.

We need to see, understand and believe that you have the skills and the focus to oversee the overwhelming details ahead. We need to believe that you understand fully and can navigate successfully all the moving parts involved with starting a company and taking that company to the finish line, meaning a highly profitable exit for investors.

Selling us on your skills should be a byproduct as you explain your idea, your plan of execution, your marketing plan, your team-building plan, and all the other areas discussed in these pages. We should hear a very focused and clear plan. We should feel confidence that you are thinking ahead of all the land mines that are coming your way and have thought through how you're going to get through them. We should feel you're on top of the details, that you know how to take chaos and organize it into a focused plan of attack. In a nutshell, we should feel in our soul that our money would be in the hands of an extremely competent person.

I said it earlier, but it's worth repeating: Investors don't really invest in the idea, the business or the exit. Although we need to see all these things and need to believe they are realistic, what we are really betting on is you — your character, abilities, confidence, humility, ethics and skills.

Remember, investors have entered a marriage-type relationship where most often we have taken a minority position. In other words, we are typically minority shareholders in a company that, in many cases, has yet to even get off the ground.

We have put ourselves in a place of trust, and in the end, this is all we have.

Let me drive this point home through my own experience. My investment history looks like this: I have invested in 39 companies. Three have been home runs. Nine have delivered solid returns. Five have been break-even. Ten are still in business, most doing well, but I have not seen any actual ROI yet. Twelve have failed.

The interesting point about my track record, however, is that all three of my home runs dramatically changed the product/service in order to succeed and out of my other successes, only half made me money with the original idea. Think about that for a minute. 100% of my home runs and half of my other successful investments were not successful with the business plan that I originally backed. Many of them had to radically alter their plan or devise new products or services to succeed. If my money was invested only in the original ideas, I would not be twice retired; I would not be writing this at all. But, fortunately, my money was invested not in a business plan, product or idea, but rather in the entrepreneurs' skill for implementation, their ability to change paths and their understanding of the market. Most importantly, my money was invested in the integrity and character of the entrepreneurs who made certain that the original investors were included, even if the winning idea was a major deviation from the original plan.

And to drive this point home even further, my investments that failed and lost me hundreds of thousands of dollars failed not because of a bad idea. They failed partly because the entrepreneurs were unable or unwilling to change with the market. Worse, a few were unethical.

For me, it all confirms the two most important investment truths:

1. **It's the character and the skill of the entrepreneur that we invest in, more so than the business plan, product or service.**
2. **If the entrepreneur is not committed to making the investors a great return, they will most certainly not get one.**

Phonies are easy to see through. Integrity, authenticity, character and your skill set are not something I can teach you. You either have them or you don't. And without these qualities, in my opinion, you probably shouldn't be raising money.

On a personal note, I am very thankful for and have ultimate respect for the entrepreneurs who I invested in that have demonstrated this high integrity and character. I would not be doing what I am doing if it were not for them.

Track Record

Seasoned investors understand the startup failure rate. They know that the reason most fail is not because the idea or timing was wrong, but rather that bad decisions were made by the founder. Bad decisions can be driven by a variety of factors: Inexperience, the wrong personality in a key role, greed, pride, distractions or questionable character, to mention a few.

In order to get a potential investor to say "yes," you must show them a track record that demonstrates that you have the character and skills needed to succeed.

You need to be able to prove to potential investors that you have done something in your past that is in the same realm as starting and running a company. Many times, investors will ask you what you've done before. If they don't, go on the offense and bring it up yourself.

There's nothing wrong with bragging about yourself in this situation when it's done for the right reasons and said in the right way. Investors want to know that you have the necessary skill set, tenacity, work ethic and leadership ability to take your venture from the drawing board to realized prosperity. As I said earlier, we are looking for proof of your skills, character and integrity. We must determine this by how you carry yourself, your business plan/offering and your past accomplishments.

If you want to increase your odds of investors saying "yes," take some extra time and outline how you are going to prove that you have these traits. I know it might feel odd to be spending so much time on yourself. You're an entrepreneur; creating a resume is a thing of the past, right? As antiquated as it sounds, a resume is what investors are looking for. Not in the traditional form, of course, but in a way that proves to us that you have the qualities and traits listed above. Most of the information can go in your business plan under what is normally called *The Management Team*, but it would do you well to spend some extra time preparing for dialogue around the experiences you have listed.

References also can go a long way. Have you made people money in the past with other businesses? Have you borrowed money and paid it back with a healthy interest? Have you headed up a department that would have failed without your leadership? Have you failed at something, but can show how you learned the lesson and got smarter as a result?

Lastly, don't forget your key team members. We need to see their "resumes," too. We won't be looking at them as closely as you, but we want to know that they are qualified to do well in their particular role.

Ultimately, the number-one product that you're selling to the investor is you. Take an honest assessment of your experience and the time to prepare your "resume" so the investor knows you have the track record for the job.

<u>Distraction-Free</u>
Starting a company and building it into a lucrative enterprise takes an enormous amount of time and focus. From my experience, the entrepreneurs with the least distractions have made me the most money. Distracted entrepreneurs most likely will struggle along without any exciting exit, sometimes even failing. Of course, there are many factors that can cause distractions: Kids, a spouse, another job, owning real estate, bills, hobbies, sports, etc.

If you are young and don't have a wife, kids or mortgage yet, you are in the perfect part of your life to start a company. For you entrepreneurs in this naturally distraction-free part of life, my advice for you is to highlight this unique ability to focus with your potential investors. This is no small thing. Letting them know that you are going to be doing nothing but trying to make their investment a success will go a long way toward raising money.

If I am catching you with a spouse, kids, mortgage, bills or some combination of these things, below are a few thoughts that might help you discuss your life situation with your potential investors:

1. Let them meet your spouse and reassure them (preferably in front of your spouse) that both of you understand that for the next few years you will be consumed by this business and not be the most attentive partner in the world.

2. If you have kids but no spouse, hire a nanny of some sort. Show us that you understand the conflict of time that will naturally arise and that you have made a plan to keep yourself focused on the business.

3. If your mortgage is a big one, downsize. When your company hits big, there will be plenty of time for the dream house.

4. Don't hide your situation. Bring it up, talk it out and show investors that you understand that starting and succeeding in this new business is all-consuming. Show them that you have a plan that will keep you totally focused.

To be fair, many investors may not specifically ask about your home situation, but from my perspective, if this is handled correctly, bringing the distraction factor to the foreground will more likely help you raise money rather than hurt your efforts. Investors know that focus is one of the critical factors, whether they bring it up or not. By answering the potential objection first, and showing your plan, it gives them another reason to invest.

Decide how to approach the discussion about the level of focus you can bring. Be honest, direct and proactive about addressing this conversation. Your strong level of commitment will help investors decide in your favor.

Want to connect with Everyday Investors who have read Todd's material?

We are envisioning *The Everyday Startup Accelerator*, where Everyday Investors virtually meet Everyday Entrepreneurs.

Jump on the waiting list at:
www.theeverydaystartupaccelerator.com
Our Pledge and Promise:

- NEVER an OBLIGATION to accept investment dollars.
- NO Junk Mail
- We will NEVER Give or Sell Your Email to anyone.
- Easy to Find "UNSUBSCRIBE" Button if you ever want to be removed from the list.

Final Thoughts

This book was written to help you raise money for your business venture in a focused and thoughtful way. Entrepreneurs frequently get overwhelmed after seeing the complexity involved in a round of fund raising.

Don't let this deter you. If you have made it this far, you are already more educated on the fundraising process than most of your competitors.

Entrepreneur and investor organizations — virtual and otherwise — are active across the country, and both national and regional events create opportunities for the two to meet and talk to each other. If you've done your research and are well prepared, these can represent an excellent means to connect with potential investors who are actively seeking opportunities.

Most of the investors in these sorts of groups are "accredited" and although you still should seek legal advice before soliciting them, they will most likely be prepared to sign a subscription agreement stating that they are accredited investors.

Since the Jobs Act passed in 2012, you now can talk with non-accredited potential investors. This is great news as it opens a sea of potential people that might invest. That said, **PLEASE BE WARNED:**

THE JOBS ACT IS COMPLICATED AND HAS MANY RULES THAT MUST BE FOLLOWED. PLEASE DO NOT SOLICIT NON-ACCREDITED INVESTORS WITHOUT CONSULTING YOUR ATTORNEY.

Put together a pitch that addresses all the main points in this book and start setting up meetings. Show up ready to go with a pitch that you know aligns yourself with the investors on the other side of the table. This will do wonders for your confidence and will do even more to further your business.

Now you know what to do. Put together your plan and do it. If you need help, find it.

The world runs on the good ideas and actions of people like you. The world needs you. We need you.

Your time is now!

All the best with your venture!

Todd E. McWhirter

ACKNOWLEDGEMENTS

I have always looked forward to this part of the writing a book... The thankful part.

Writing does not come natural for me; therefore, I have many people to thank. My mother, a retired teacher, read each book multiple times finding and correcting grammar errors. More importantly, she kept believing in me. Thank you, Mom!! My Dad, from early on, helped me understand money- both how to save and how to think about it. Thank you, Dad! My girlfriend, Tammie, of 14 years stuck with me through my loss of everything. Thankfully she kept believing I would land on my feet. She's a goof ball - calls me Teeter Todder - and likes to say "teeter todders but he doesn't fall down". Thank you, Tammie, for believing in me! My kids, Ethan and Ellie, were huge supporters, asking me questions, interested in my progress, throwing their 2 cents in on cover choices, etc. They keep me motivated in so many ways it's hard to even quantify. Thank you, Ethan! Thank you, Ellie! A big thank you to Dave Ness, Doug Horch and Brian Grayson for encouraging and helping me early on, back when we were calling it the 50X project – great memories!

The book(s) would not be the same without Nate Warren and Durand Achée, my editors. So much time we all spent going over the details. Thank you Both! I wrote these pages by locking myself down at a coffee shop each morning, not leaving until I finished 3 hours of work. That place was *The Bike Café* in Denver Colorado. Thank you Jess and Peter for creating such a great atmosphere and welcoming me personally each morning for all that time. Without the amazing entrepreneurs and the loyal investors who came along side some of my good decisions and bad decisions, none of the content would have ever came to pass. Some are mentioned in the stories I tell, some are not, there are many and you know who you are. Thank you so very much! And finally, I want to thank all my friends and family who supported me in the process, voting on covers, giving thoughts on content, adding so much value and helping with those little things that as we know are the big things. There are many of you, and again, you know who you are. Sincerely, Thank you!!

ABOUT THE AUTHOR

Following an impressive 14-year career in sales and sales management, **Todd E. McWhirter** transitioned into an Angel Investor almost by accident. He likes to call himself the "accidental startup investor", yet through his hands-on experience evaluating over 400 startups over the past 23 years, McWhirter has developed a proven and practical methodology that resulted in 39 startup investments that have generated a remarkable 7X overall return, growing his investment dollars from thousands to multi-millions.

Through years of comprehensive experience, including dramatic wins, bankruptcy and an amazing come back, McWhirter documented what worked and what did not. He turned these notes into two books: one for entrepreneurs looking to raise capital – *Funding Your Startup* – and one for everyday people, just like himself, to begin investing in startup companies – *The Everyday Startup Investor.*

More than anything, this accidental investor is a team player who wants to help everyone around him succeed. With the JOBS Act finally making it legal for non-accredited investors to participate in funding emerging growth companies, his passion to guide and support others in this exciting entrepreneurial adventure is expressed in these two books.

www.ingramcontent.com/pod-product-compliance
Lightning Source LLC
Chambersburg PA
CBHW020157200326
41521CB00006B/411